CW00486846

Contents

General Knowledge

1) Who scored the club's first ever Premier League hat-trick in the match versus Sunderland in April 2015?

2) Which club beat Palace on aggregate in the 2006 Championship Play-Off Semi Final?

3) Who scored 30 goals for the club in the 2012/13 Championship season?

4) Tony Popovic scored his infamous flicked own goal against which team in September 2004?

5) Who saw his penalty saved by Karl Darlow as Palace lost 1-0 away to Newcastle in April 2016?

6) Which Charlton player scored late on to snatch a draw and relegate Palace from the Premier League in 2005?

7) Which striker had come off the bench to score and then win a penalty which looked to have ensured survival in the same match?

8) Who was the clubs top scorer in the First Division with 22 goals in the 2001/02 season?

9) Against which team did Wilfried Zaha make his Crystal Palace debut in March 2010?

10) Who became the first Uruguayan to play for the club after signing in 2004?

11) Who made his debut for the club aged just 15 against Watford in October 2007?

12) Who became the clubs oldest Premier League player when he played against Fulham in October 2013?

13) Bristol City beat Palace in the Championship Play-Off Semi-Final in which year?

14) Which Brighton player was sent off in stoppage time during the 1-1 draw between the sides in October 2020?

15) Which squad number has Martin Kelly worn since signing in 2014?

16) Who did Frank de Boer name as the new permanent club captain in July 2017?

17) Who scored an own-goal as Crystal Palace lost 1-0 at home to Sheffield United in February 2020?

18) How many goals did Andrew Johnson score in the 2004/05 Premier League season?

19) Which company was the club's main shirt sponsor for the 2004/05 Premier League season?

20) In which year were the club docked 10 points after going into administration?

21) Palace secured a 0-0 draw with Burnley in September 2014 when which goalkeeper saved a late penalty from Burnley's Scott Arfield?

22) Palace won 3-1 at Old Trafford in September 2020, partly thanks to a penalty scored by Zaha, but who had missed the initial penalty before a re-take was ordered?

23) Palace beat Brighton 5-0 in October 2002, but who was in charge of the visitors that day?

Transfers 2000-2009

1) Forward Mathias Svensson was sold to which club in January 2000?

2) From which team did Crystal Palace buy Julian Gray in July 2000?

3) Which English centre-back signed from West Ham in the summer of 2000?

4) From which side was Dougie Freedman purchased in October 2000?

5) Defender Andy Linighan left to sign permanently for which club in October 2000?

6) Who arrived from Japanese club Sanfrecce Hiroshima in the summer of 2001?

7) Danny Granville was bought from which team in December 2001?

8) Which striker came in from Leicester City in February 2002?

9) From which club did Palace buy Andrew Johnson in July 2002?

10) Striker Clinton Morrison was sold to which team in July 2002?

11) Shaun Derry was purchased from which side in August 2002?

12) Which two players did Palace sign from Wimbledon in the summer of 2003?

13) From which German club did goalkeeper Gabor Kiraly arrive in July 2004?

14) Palace also signed goalkeeper Julian Speroni in July 2004, which Scottish club was he bought from?

15) Which defender arrived from Southampton in August of 2004?

16) Who was Wayne Routledge sold to in July 2005?

17) Neil Shipperley signed for which club on a free transfer in July 2005?

18) Palace bought which defender from Hull City in June 2006?

19) From which club did forward Jamie Scowcroft arrive in July 2006?

20) Which striker was bought from Blackburn Rovers in the summer of 2006?

21) Jobi McAnuff was sold to which team in June 2007?

22) Clint Hill signed for Palace from which side in January 2008?

23) From which team was Patrick McCarthy purchased in June 2008?

24) Which two players were sold to Millwall in January 2008?

25) Defender Jose Fonte arrived from which Portuguese club in 2008?

26) Which young midfield player was sold to Tottenham in July 2008?

27) Which central midfielder was sold to Wigan in January 2009?

28) Striker Stern John arrived in July 2009 from which club?

Cup Games

1) Palace were knocked out of the FA Cup at the Third Round stage in 2020 by which side?

2) Which lower-league side knocked Palace out of the League Cup on penalties in 2019?

3) Which team did Crystal Palace beat 7-0 in the League Cup in October 2002?

4) Liverpool were beaten at Anfield in the FA Cup Fourth Round Replay in 2003 by what score?

5) Which team did Palace beat on penalties in the League Cup in 2001?

6) Who was the unlikely scorer of a hat-trick in the 3-1 win over Wolves in the FA Cup Fourth Round Replay in February 2010?

7) Palace lost to Liverpool on aggregate in the league Cup Semi Final of 2001, losing the second leg 5-0 at Anfield after having previously won at home by what score?

8) Which team knocked Palace out of the FA Cup in both 2006 and 2007?

9) Who scored the Manchester United winner in extra time as Crystal Palace were beaten 2-1 in the 2016 FA Cup final?

10) Palace beat Tottenham Hotspur 1-0 away from home in the FA Cup Fifth Round of 2016, who scored the only goal of the game?

11) Palace reached the League Cup Semi-Final by beating Manchester United 2-1 at Old Trafford in November 2011 thanks to goals from Glenn Murray and a long-range screamer from which player?

12) Which club were Palace then beaten by on penalties in the Semi-Final?

Memorable Games

1) Palace beat Watford 1-0 in the 2013
   Play-Off Final thanks to a Kevin Phillips
   penalty, but who won the spot kick?

2) Neil Shipperley scored the only goal as
   Palace beat West Ham in the Play-Off
   Final to secure promotion to the Premier
   League in which year?

3) Bournemouth were beaten 5-3 on the
   last day of the 2018/19 season, who
   scored a brace for Palace that day?

4) Which team did Crystal Palace beat 1-0
   on the last day of the 2000/01 season to
   avoid relegation to Division Two?

5) Palace ensured Championship survival
   on the last day of the 2009/10 season
   and also relegated their opponents
   Sheffield Wednesday, what was the final
   score?

6) Crystal Palace beat Brighton in the Championship Play-Off Semi Finals in 2013, which player scored the two goals to secure the win?

7) Liverpool squandered a three goal lead to draw 3-3 at Selhurst Park and damage their title bid, but which Palace player sparked the come-back with a deflected long-range effort?

8) Which team did Palace beat 5-0 at home in the Premier League in April 2018?

9) Who scored a hat-trick as Ipswich Town were beaten 5-0 at Selhurst Park in November 2012?

10) Who scored the late winner to secure a 2-1 win at Old Trafford in August 2019?

11) Which Manchester City player scored a late own goal to gift Palace a 2-2 draw at the Etihad in January 2020?

12) Palace won 3-2 at Brighton in November 2005, which player scored his 100th goal for the club during the match?

13) Who scored the late winner as Palace won 3-2 away to Brighton in November 2005?

Memorable Goals

1) Which Palace player scored the Premier League goal of the month for December 2018?

2) Jordan Ayew scored a brilliant individual goal to secure a last-minute 2-1 win over which team in December 2019?

3) Who opened the scoring in the 2-0 FA Cup win at Anfield in February 2003 with a stunning long-range strike?

4) Eberechi Eze scored a fine solo effort after running from inside his own half to net against which team in a 2-0 win in January 2021?

5) Who scored the winner as Palace beat Manchester United for the first time in the Premier League, with a 2-1 victory at Old Trafford in August 2019?

6) Which defender scored the winner against Liverpool at Anfield in the 2-1 win in November 2015?

7) Dougie Freedman scored a last minute equaliser with a left footed volley against which side in November 2006?

8) Jamie Scowcroft netted with a long-range volley away from home against which team in January 2008?

9) Yohan Cabaye scored with a beautiful looping effort against Arsenal in April 2017, but what was the final score of the game?

10) Who scored the club's first goal back in the Premier League in 2004 in the 1-1 draw away to Norwich City?

Starting XI

Can you name the starting team for the 2004 Play-Off Final win against West Ham from the initials given?

N. V
D. B
T. P
M. L
D. G
W. R
A. R
S. D
M. H
N. S
A. J

Red Cards

1) Which defender was sent off during the 2-2 draw with Southampton in May 2005?

2) Palace held on for a 0-0 draw at home to Manchester United in March 2005 despite seeing which player dismissed for two bookable offences?

3) Yannick Bolasie was sent off in the 1-0 win over which side in November 2013?

4) Who scored twice but was then sent off in the 3-1 win away at West Ham in February 2015?

5) Palace lost 3-1 at home to West Ham in the October of 2015 after which player received two yellow cards?

6) Wilfried Zaha saw red against which team in January 2019?

7) What was unusual about the red card shown to Christian Benteke during the visit to Villa Park in July 2020?

8) Captain Neil Ruddock was sent off at home to which side in a 1-0 defeat in Division One in September 2000?

9) Which winger was dismissed in the 3-3 draw with Watford in September 2002?

10) Which Palace player was shown a red card after a VAR review in the FA Cup tie with Derby County in January 2020?

11) Both teams finished with ten men as Chelsea won 2-1 at Selhurst Park in October 2014, but who was sent off for the hosts?

12) Claude Davis was sent off during a 1-0 home loss to which side in the Championship in March 2010?

Managers

1) Who was Crystal Palace manager at the beginning of the 21st Century?

2) Who were the opponents for Iain Dowie's last game as manager?

3) Who replaced Iain Dowie as manager in 2006?

4) Alan Pardew faced which team in the FA Cup Third Round in his first game as Crystal Palace manager?

5) Dougie Freedman took over as manager from who in January 2011?

6) Freedman took over as manager of which club after leaving Palace in October 2012?

7) How many games did Frank de Boer take charge of as Crystal Palace manager?

8) Roy Hodgson lost his first match in charge 1-0 at home against which team?

9) In what year did Neil Warnock return for his second spell as manager?

10) Which manager led Palace back to the Premier League with promotion in the 2012/13 season?

Starting XI (2)

Can you name the starting team for the 2016 FA Cup Final loss versus Manchester United from the initials given?

W. H

J. W

S. D

D. D

P. S

M. J

J. M

W. Z

Y. C

Y. B

C. W

First Goals – Can you name the teams that these players scored their first goal for the club against?

1) Wilfried Zaha

2) Jordan Ayew

3) Christian Benteke

4) Kevin Phillips

5) Andrew Johnson

6) Yannick Bolasie

7) Clinton Morrison

8) Dougie Freedman

9) Neil Shipperley

10) Luka Milivojevic

11) Andros Townsend

12) Joel Ward

13) Shaun Derry

14) Darren Ambrose

15) Glenn Murray

16) Fraizer Campbell

17) Eberechi Eze

18) Gary Cahill

Transfers 2010-2021

1) Victor Moses left the club in the winter transfer window of 2010 to sign for which club?

2) Danny Butterfield left Crystal Palace permanently in July 2010 to sign for which side?

3) Glenn Murray signed on a free transfer from which team in May 2011?

4) Who was signed from Turkish club Genclerbirligi in July 2001?

5) Goalkeeper Wes Foderingham left to sign for which club in January 2012?

6) Joel Ward was bought from which club in the summer of 2012?

7) From which club was winger Yannick Bolasie purchased in August 2012?

8) Which midfielder was sold to Birmingham City in July 2012?

9) Who was sold to Manchester United in January 2013?

10) From which club did Palace sign Dwight Gayle in July 2013?

11) Which two players arrived permanently from Blackpool in the summer of 2013?

12) Which centre back signed on a free from Fulham in 2014?

13) Which central midfielder was brought in from PSG in 2015?

14) From which club was striker Connor Wickham purchased in August 2015?

15) Palace signed which midfield player from Arsenal on a free in September 2016?

16) Jairo Riedewald arrived from which Dutch club in July 2017?

17) Goalkeeper Steve Mandanda left the club in July 2017 to join which French side?

18) From which club did Palace buy Cheikhou Kouyate in 2018?

19) Midfielder Jonny Williams left Crystal Palace permanently in January 2019 to sign for which club?

20) Which midfielder was bought from Everton in August 2019?

21) For which team did Jason Puncheon sign after leaving Palace in 2019

22) Midfielder Eberechi Eze was signed from which Championship club in August 2020?

23) Which German player was released from his contract in January 2021?

Answers

General Knowledge Answers

1) Who scored the club's first ever Premier League hat-trick in the match versus Sunderland in April 2015?
Yannick Bolasie

2) Which club beat Palace on aggregate in the 2006 Championship Play-Off Semi Final?
Watford

3) Who scored 30 goals for the club in the 2012/13 Championship season?
Glenn Murray

4) Tony Popovic scored his infamous flicked own goal against which team in September 2004?
Portsmouth

5) Who saw his penalty saved by Karl Darlow as Palace lost 1-0 away to Newcastle in April 2016?
Yohan Cabaye

6) Which Charlton player scored late on to snatch a draw and relegate Palace from the Premier League in 2005?
Jonathan Fortune

7) Which striker had come off the bench to score and then win a penalty which looked to have ensured survival in the same match?
Dougie Freedman

8) Who was the clubs top scorer in the First Division with 22 goals in the 2001/02 season?
Clinton Morrison

9) Against which team did Wilfried Zaha make his Crystal Palace debut in March 2010?
Cardiff City

10) Who became the first Uruguayan to play for the club after signing in 2004?
Gonzalo Sorondo

11) Who made his debut for the club aged just 15 against Watford in October 2007?
John Bostock

12) Who became the clubs oldest Premier League player when he played against Fulham in October 2013?
Kevin Phillips

13) Bristol City beat Palace in the Championship Play-Off Semi-Final in which year?
2008

14) Which Brighton player was sent off in stoppage time during the 1-1 draw between the sides in October 2020?
Lewis Dunk

15) Which squad number has Martin Kelly worn since signing in 2014?
34

16) Who did Frank de Boer name as the new permanent club captain in July 2017?
Jason Puncheon

17) Who scored an own-goal as Crystal Palace lost 1-0 at home to Sheffield United in February 2020?
Vicente Guaita

18) How many goals did Andrew Johnson score in the 2004/05 Premier League season?
21

19) Which company was the club's main shirt sponsor for the 2004/05 Premier League season?
Churchill

20) In which year were the club docked 10 points after going into administration?
2010

21) Palace secured a 0-0 draw with Burnley in September 2014 when which goalkeeper saved a late penalty from Burnley's Scott Arfield?
Julian Speroni

22) Palace won 3-1 at Old Trafford in September 2020, partly thanks to a penalty scored by Zaha, but who had missed the initial penalty before a re-take was ordered?
Jordan Ayew

23) Palace beat Brighton 5-0 in October 2002, but who was in charge of the visitors that day?
Steve Coppell

Transfers 2000-2009 Answers

1) Forward Mathias Svensson was sold to which club in January 2000?
Charlton Athletic

2) From which team did Crystal Palace buy Julian Gray in July 2000?
Arsenal

3) Which English centre-back signed from West Ham in the summer of 2000?
Neil Ruddock

4) From which side was Dougie Freedman purchased in October 2000?
Nottingham Forest

5) Defender Andy Linighan left to sign permanently for which club in October 2000?
Oxford United

6) Who arrived from Japanese club Sanfrecce Hiroshima in the summer of 2001?
Tony Popovic

7) Danny Granville was bought from which team in December 2001?
Manchester City

8) Which striker came in from Leicester City in February 2002?
Ade Akinbiyi

9) From which club did Palace buy Andrew Johnson in July 2002?
Birmingham City

10) Striker Clinton Morrison was sold to which team in July 2002?
Birmingham City

11) Shaun Derry was purchased from which side in August 2002?
Portsmouth

12) Which two players did Palace sign from Wimbledon in the summer of 2003?
Neil Shipperley and Michael Hughes

13) From which German club did goalkeeper Gabor Kiraly arrive in July 2004?
Hertha Berlin

14) Palace also signed goalkeeper Julian Speroni in July 2004, which Scottish club was he bought from?
Dundee

15) Which defender arrived from Southampton in August of 2004?
Fitz Hall

16) Who was Wayne Routledge sold to in July 2005?
Tottenham Hotspur

17) Neil Shipperley signed for which club on a free transfer in July 2005?
Sheffield United

18) Palace bought which defender from Hull City in June 2006?

Leon Cort

19) From which club did forward Jamie Scowcroft arrive in July 2006?

Coventry City

20) Which striker was bought from Blackburn Rovers in the summer of 2006?

Shefki Kuqi

21) Jobi McAnuff was sold to which team in June 2007?

Watford

22) Clint Hill signed for Palace from which side in January 2008?

Stoke City

23) From which team was Patrick McCarthy purchased in June 2008?

Charlton Athletic

24) Which two players were sold to Millwall in January 2008?
Lewis Grabban and Dave Martin

25) Defender Jose Fonte arrived from which Portuguese club in 2008?
Benfica

26) Which young midfield player was sold to Tottenham in July 2008?
John Bostock

27) Which central midfielder was sold to Wigan in January 2009?
Ben Watson

28) Striker Stern John arrived in July 2009 from which club?
Southampton

Cup Games Answers

1) Palace were knocked out of the FA Cup at the Third Round stage in 2020 by which side?
Derby County

2) Which lower-league side knocked Palace out of the League Cup on penalties in 2019?
Colchester United

3) Which team did Crystal Palace beat 7-0 in the League Cup in October 2002?
Cheltenham Town

4) Liverpool were beaten at Anfield in the FA Cup Fourth Round Replay in 2003 by what score?
2-0

5) Which team did Palace beat on penalties in the League Cup in 2001?
Everton

6) Who was the unlikely scorer of a hat-trick in the 3-1 win over Wolves in the FA Cup Fourth Round Replay in February 2010?
Danny Butterfield

7) Palace lost to Liverpool on aggregate in the league Cup Semi Final of 2001, losing the second leg 5-0 at Anfield after having previously won at home by what score?
2-1

8) Which team knocked Palace out of the FA Cup in both 2006 and 2007?
Preston North End

9) Who scored the Manchester United winner in extra time as Crystal Palace were beaten 2-1 in the 2016 FA Cup final?
Jesse Lingard

10) Palace beat Tottenham Hotspur 1-0 away from home in the FA Cup Fifth Round of 2016, who scored the only goal of the game?
Martin Kelly

11) Palace reached the League Cup Semi-Final by beating Manchester United 2-1 at Old Trafford in November 2011 thanks to goals from Glenn Murray and a long-range screamer from which player?
Darren Ambrose

12) Which club were Palace then beaten by on penalties in the Semi-Final?
Cardiff City

Memorable Games Answers

1) Palace beat Watford 1-0 in the 2013 Play-Off Final thanks to a Kevin Phillips penalty, but who won the spot kick?
Wilfried Zaha

2) Neil Shipperley scored the only goal as Palace beat West Ham in the Play-Off Final to secure promotion to the Premier League in which year?
2004

3) Bournemouth were beaten 5-3 on the last day of the 2018/19 season, who scored a brace for Palace that day?
Michy Batshuayi

4) Which team did Crystal Palace beat 1-0 on the last day of the 2000/01 season to avoid relegation to Division Two?
Stockport County

5) Palace ensured Championship survival on the last day of the 2009/10 season and also relegated their opponents Sheffield Wednesday, what was the final score?
2-2

6) Crystal Palace beat Brighton in the Championship Play-Off Semi Finals in 2013, which player scored the two goals to secure the win?
Wilfried Zaha

7) Liverpool squandered a three goal lead to draw 3-3 at Selhurst Park and damage their title bid, but which Palace player sparked the come-back with a deflected long-range effort?
Damien Delaney

8) Which team did Palace beat 5-0 at home in the Premier League in April 2018?
Leicester City

9) Who scored a hat-trick as Ipswich Town were beaten 5-0 at Selhurst Park in November 2012?
Glenn Murray

10) Who scored the late winner to secure a 2-1 win at Old Trafford in August 2019?
Patrick Van Aanholt

11) Which Manchester City player scored a late own goal to gift Palace a 2-2 draw at the Etihad in January 2020?
Fernandinho

12) Palace won 3-2 at Brighton in November 2005, which player scored his 100th goal for the club during the match?
Dougie Freedman

13) Who scored the late winner as Palace won 3-2 away to Brighton in November 2005?
Jobi McAnuff

Memorable Goals Answers

1) Which Palace player scored the Premier
   League goal of the month for December
   2018?
   Andros Townsend

2) Jordan Ayew scored a brilliant individual
   goal to secure a last-minute 2-1 win
   over which team in December 2019?
   West Ham

3) Who opened the scoring in the 2-0 FA
   Cup win at Anfield in February 2003 with
   a stunning long-range strike?
   Julian Gray

4) Eberechi Eze scored a fine solo effort
   after running from inside his own half to
   net against which team in a 2-0 win in
   January 2021?
   Sheffield United

5) Who scored the winner as Palace beat Manchester United for the first time in the Premier League, with a 2-1 victory at Old Trafford in August 2019?
Patrick van Aanholt

6) Which defender scored the winner against Liverpool at Anfield in the 2-1 win in November 2015?
Scott Dann

7) Dougie Freedman scored a last minute equaliser with a left footed volley against which side in November 2006?
Wolverhampton Wanderers

8) Jamie Scowcroft netted with a long-range volley away from home against which team in January 2008?
Wolverhampton Wanderers

9) Yohan Cabaye scored with a beautiful looping effort against Arsenal in April 2017, but what was the final score of the game?
Crystal Palace 3-0 Arsenal

10) Who scored the club's first goal back in the Premier League in 2004 in the 1-1 draw away to Norwich City?
Andrew Johnson

Starting XI Answers

Can you name the starting team for the 2004 Play-Off Final win against West Ham from the initials given?

Nico Vaesen
Danny Butterfield
Tony Popovic
Mikele Leigertwood
Danny Granville
Wayne Routledge
Aki Riihilahti
Shaun Derry
Michael Hughes
Neil Shipperley
Andrew Johnson

Red Cards Answers

1) Which defender was sent off during the 2-2 draw with Southampton in May 2005?
Gonzalo Sorondo

2) Palace held on for a 0-0 draw at home to Manchester United in March 2005 despite seeing which player dismissed for two bookable offences?
Vassilis Lakis

3) Yannick Bolasie was sent off in the 1-0 win over which side in November 2013?
Hull City

4) Who scored twice but was then sent off in the 3-1 win away at West Ham in February 2015?
Glenn Murray

5) Palace lost 3-1 at home to West Ham in the October of 2015 after which player received two yellow cards?
Dwight Gayle

6) Wilfried Zaha saw red against which team in January 2019?
Southampton

7) What was unusual about the red card shown to Christian Benteke during the visit to Villa Park in July 2020?
It was given after full-time

8) Captain Neil Ruddock was sent off at home to which side in a 1-0 defeat in Division One in September 2000?
Sheffield United

9) Which winger was dismissed in the 3-3 draw with Watford in September 2002?
Wayne Routledge

10) Which Palace player was shown a red card after a VAR review in the FA Cup tie with Derby County in January 2020?
Luka Milivojevic

11) Both teams finished with ten men as Chelsea won 2-1 at Selhurst Park in October 2014, but who was sent off for the hosts?
Damien Delaney

12) Claude Davis was sent off during a 1-0 home loss to which side in the Championship in March 2010?
Leicester City

Managers Answers

1) Who was Crystal Palace manager at the beginning of the 21st Century?
Steve Coppell

2) Who were the opponents for Iain Dowie's last game as manager?
Watford

3) Who replaced Iain Dowie as manager in 2006?
Peter Taylor

4) Alan Pardew faced which team in the FA Cup Third Round in his first game as Crystal Palace manager?
Dover Athletic

5) Dougie Freedman took over as manager from who in January 2011?
George Burley

6) Freedman took over as manager of which club after leaving Palace in October 2012?
Bolton Wanderers

7) How many games did Frank de Boer take charge of as Crystal Palace manager?
Five

8) Roy Hodgson lost his first match in charge 1-0 at home against which team?
Southampton

9) In what year did Neil Warnock return for his second spell as manager?
2014

10) Which manager led Palace back to the Premier League with promotion in the 2012/13 season?
Ian Holloway

Starting XI (2) Answers

Can you name the starting team for the 2016 FA Cup Final loss versus Manchester United from the initials given?

Wayne Hennessey
Joel Ward
Scott Dann
Damien Delaney
Pape Souare
Mile Jedinak
James McArthur
Wilfried Zaha
Yohan Cabaye
Yannick Bolasie
Connor Wickham

First Goals Answers

1) Wilfried Zaha
   Leicester City

2) Jordan Ayew
   Wolverhampton Wanderers

3) Christian Benteke
   Middlesbrough

4) Kevin Phillips
   Hull City

5) Andrew Johnson
   Wimbledon

6) Yannick Bolasie
   Ipswich Town

7) Clinton Morrison
   Coventry City

8) Dougie Freedman
   Rotherham

9) Neil Shipperley
Sheffield Wednesday

10) Luka Milivojevic
Arsenal

11) Andros Townsend
Stoke City

12) Joel Ward
QPR

13) Shaun Derry
Grimsby Town

14) Darren Ambrose
Torquay United

15) Glenn Murray
Blackpool

16) Fraizer Campbell
Everton

17) Eberechi Eze
   Leeds United

18) Gary Cahill
   Newcastle United

Transfers 2010-2020 Answers

1) Victor Moses left the club in the winter transfer window of 2010 to sign for which club?
Wigan

2) Danny Butterfield left Crystal Palace permanently in July 2010 to sign for which side?
Southampton

3) Glenn Murray signed on a free transfer from which team in May 2011?
Brighton

4) Who was signed from Turkish club Genclerbirligi in July 2001?
Mile Jedinak

5) Goalkeeper Wes Foderingham left to sign for which club in January 2012?
Swindon Town

6) Joel Ward was bought from which club in the summer of 2012?
Portsmouth

7) From which club was winger Yannick Bolasie purchased in August 2012?
Bristol City

8) Which midfielder was sold to Birmingham City in July 2012?
Darren Ambrose

9) Who was sold to Manchester United in January 2013?
Wilfried Zaha

10) From which club did Palace sign Dwight Gayle in July 2013?
Peterborough

11) Which two players arrived permanently from Blackpool in the summer of 2013?
Kevin Phillips and Elliott Grandin

12) Which centre back signed on a free from Fulham in 2014?
Brede Hangeland

13) Which central midfielder was brought in from PSG in 2015?
Yohan Cabaye

14) From which club was striker Connor Wickham purchased in August 2015?
Sunderland

15) Palace signed which midfield player from Arsenal on a free in September 2016?
Mathieu Flamini

16) Jairo Riedewald arrived from which Dutch club in July 2017?
Ajax

17) Goalkeeper Steve Mandanda left the club in July 2017 to join which French side?
Marseille

18) From which club did Palace buy Cheikhou Kouyate in 2018?
West Ham

19) Midfielder Jonny Williams left Crystal Palace permanently in January 2019 to sign for which club?
Charlton Athletic

20) Which midfielder was bought from Everton in August 2019?
James McCarthy

21) For which team did Jason Puncheon sign after leaving Palace in 2019?
Pafos

22) Midfielder Eberechi Eze was signed from which Championship club in August 2020?
QPR

23) Which German player was released from his contract in January 2021?
Max Meyer

If you enjoyed this book please consider leaving a five star review on Amazon

Books by Jack Pearson available on Amazon:

Cricket:

Cricket World Cup 2019 Quiz Book
The Ashes 2019 Cricket Quiz Book
The Ashes 2010-2019 Quiz Book
The Ashes 2005 Quiz Book
The Indian Premier League Quiz Book

Football:

The Quiz Book of the England Football Team in the 21st Century
The Quiz Book of Arsenal Football Club in the 21st Century
The Quiz Book of Aston Villa Football Club in the 21st Century
The Quiz Book of Chelsea Football Club in the 21st Century

The Quiz Book of Everton Football Club in the 21st Century

The Quiz Book of Leeds United Football Club in the 21st Century

The Quiz Book of Leicester City Football Club in the 21st Century

The Quiz Book of Liverpool Football Club in the 21st Century

The Quiz Book of Manchester City Football Club in the 21st Century

The Quiz Book of Manchester United Football Club in the 21st Century

The Quiz Book of Newcastle United Football Club in the 21st Century

The Quiz Book of Southampton Football Club in the 21st Century

The Quiz Book of Sunderland Association Football Club in the 21st Century

The Quiz Book of Tottenham Hotspur Football Club in the 21st Century

The Quiz Book of West Ham United Football Club in the 21st Century

The Quiz Book of Wrexham Association Football Club in the 21st Century

Printed in Great Britain
by Amazon